STRONG, HEALTHY GIRLS

COPING WITH STRESS AND PRESSURE

By Carrie Myers

CONTENT CONSULTANT

Jenny Oliphant, EdD, MPH
Community Outreach Coordinator and Research Associate
Healthy Youth Development-Prevention Research Center
University of Minnesota
School of Medicine, Division of General Pediatrics and Adolescent Health

Essential Library
An Imprint of Abdo Publishing | abdobooks.com

abdobooks.com

Published by Abdo Publishing, a division of ABDO, PO Box 398166, Minneapolis, Minnesota 55439. Copyright © 2021 by Abdo Consulting Group, Inc. International copyrights reserved in all countries. No part of this book may be reproduced in any form without written permission from the publisher. Essential Library™ is a trademark and logo of Abdo Publishing.

Printed in the United States of America, North Mankato, Minnesota.
082020
012021

Cover Photo: Shutterstock Images
Interior Photos: iStockphoto, 8, 12, 14–15, 18, 24–25, 26–27, 30, 33, 40, 42–43, 52, 56–57, 58–59, 64, 66–67, 72–73, 88; Syda Productions/Shutterstock Images, 11; SDI Productions/iStockphoto, 21; Way Home Studio/Shutterstock Images, 22–23; Evgeniy Shkolenko/iStockphoto, 36–37; Antonio Guillem/iStockphoto, 45, 47; DME Photography/iStockphoto, 48–49; Prostock–Studio/iStockphoto, 54–55; Wave Break Media/iStockphoto, 60; Martin Dimitrov/iStockphoto, 68–69; Juan Monino/iStockphoto, 76; Shutterstock Images, 78–79, 90, 92–93; Juan Monino/iStockphoto, 81; Prostock–Studio/iStockphoto, 84; Bernard Bobo/iStockphoto, 96–97; Yakobchuk Viacheslav/Shutterstock Images, 98–99

Editor: Melissa York
Series Designer: Nikki Nordby

Library of Congress Control Number: 2019954371
Publisher's Cataloging-in-Publication Data

Names: Myers, Carrie, author.
Title: Coping with stress and pressure / by Carrie Myers
Description: Minneapolis, Minnesota : Abdo Publishing, 2021 | Series: Strong, healthy girls | Includes online resources and index.
Identifiers: ISBN 9781532192142 (lib. bdg.) | ISBN 9781098210045 (ebook)
Subjects: LCSH: Teenage girls--Psychology--Juvenile literature. | Everyday living skills--Juvenile literature. | Coping behavior--Juvenile literature. | Stress in adolescence--Juvenile literature. | Expectancies of self-efficacy--Juvenile literature.
Classification: DDC 155.533--dc23

CONTENTS

DR. JENNY

Jenny Oliphant believes all young people deserve to thrive, not just survive. Her work focuses on making sure parents, professionals, and young people themselves have the information, skills, and tools to make that happen. She's an expert in adolescent sexual health, youth development, health education, and sports education.

Dr. Jenny holds a master's of public health in community health education from the University of Minnesota and a doctorate from the University of Saint Thomas in educational leadership. She speaks locally and nationally about youth development, peer education, and pregnancy prevention. Her background includes experiences as a health educator and adjunct instructor in health for community health educators, health teachers, and epidemiologists in training.

Dr. Jenny is the community outreach coordinator and research associate for the Healthy Youth Development-Prevention Research Center at the University of Minnesota in the School of Medicine, Division of General Pediatrics and Adolescent Health. There, she helps families and health providers design and implement youth-friendly health programming supported by current research. At Walden University, as a contributing faculty member, she teaches students the art and science of becoming community-engaged public health professionals working for social change.

Dr. Jenny teaches future pediatricians and nurses how to interview teens about their sexual health. She recently wrapped up a five-year study in which she worked with middle schools to develop teaching plans to improve students' social and emotional health. Her newest research is focused on helping clinics better engage with adolescent patients. She's also working on training dentists and hygienists to recommend the human papillomavirus vaccine to parents and young people.

Dr. Jenny has worked as a consultant for a series of books written for teens and focused on topics in adolescent health. She's also served as a federal accuracy reviewer for numerous curricula used in programming funded by the US government's Office of Adolescent Health.

She lives in Minneapolis, Minnesota, with her teen children, her husband, and her bulldog, Sid. In the future, she dreams of living and working in Berlin, Germany, and continues to practice her German, in hopes of making her dream come true.

TAKE IT

FROM ME

If you're a typical teenager, you likely face stress in many areas of your life—navigating the emotional and physical ups and downs of adolescence, finding your identity, making decisions about your future, and facing your fears in relationships, the classroom, on stage, or on the field. You may be dealing with pressure from teachers, parents, friends, significant others, and even from yourself.

The good news is that every teen has the opportunity to learn positive ways to respond to difficult situations, thoughts, and emotions. As you read through the following stories, you may find similarities to your own experiences or the experiences of your peers. I hope you'll be able to see yourself in some of these teenagers and to take away strategies to manage your own stress, promote healthy attitudes, and thrive in mind, body, and soul.

There are times, though, when you or your peers might experience worry, fears, or sadness that feel way beyond what you can manage. Anxiety and depression are clinical conditions that need to be addressed by a mental health professional. The same is especially true for self-harming behaviors or suicidal thoughts or actions. If you suspect that someone is in danger of causing harm to themselves, please get immediate help. Call 911, go to an emergency room, or call the National Suicide Prevention Lifeline at 1-800-723-TALK (8522). Always take thoughts of or plans for suicide seriously.

As both the parent of an almost-adult and as someone who has survived adolescence, I can promise you that it's possible to survive and thrive as you journey toward adulthood. As you read and learn more about how to handle stress in healthy ways, I hope you're encouraged by what you learn about your changing body and mind and the exciting stage of life you're in now: a time when you're as smart and as full of possibility as you've ever been.

SINCERELY,
CARRIE

CHAPTER ONE

ALIEN INVASION

Remember when you were a child and life felt simpler? You played with your friends and didn't have to do much homework. If you did happen to feel grumpy, usually a nap and a snack took care of everything. What happened to those days?

If you're like most teenage girls, sometime around the age of 12 life suddenly gets a lot more complicated. Your body starts to change and doesn't stop. You start menstruating. You buy a bra. Your group of friends turns into the cast of a soapy drama, except with more acne and braces and, for the boys, squeaky voices and scraggly almost-mustaches. You get into fights with your parents. You may feel like you're always angry, sad, sleep deprived, unhappy with your appearance, embarrassed, anxious, emotional, stressed out, or crying. Your feelings can be unpredictable, powerful, and often excruciating.

Pressure to succeed at school and at life might seem to come from every direction.

Jordan had a day where all the complications of being a teen seemed to hit her all at once. Read her story to find out how she handled it.

JORDAN'S STORY

Jordan woke up with the biggest pimple she'd ever seen. Multiple layers of concealer, powder, and foundation—even the expensive department store brand she borrowed from her mom—did nothing to hide it. "It looks like I have a third eye on my forehead," she grumbled. It was going to be one of those days.

Sure enough, before school even started, Jordan had a fight with her best friend, Lily. Jordan had no idea how it even started. One minute, they were gossiping about the upcoming Winter Ball and whom they wanted to ask. The next thing Jordan knew, Lily was red faced and crying. "You're so selfish! You never think about anyone but yourself!" she bawled.

TALK ABOUT IT

■ Have you ever felt as though your life and emotions were out of your control? What led you to feel that way? What was the experience like?

■ Have you ever found yourself in an emotional argument with a friend? What was the argument about? Were you able to understand your friend's point of view? Why or why not?

■ What changes in your body have you noticed since you've entered adolescence? Which changes have you enjoyed the most? The least?

Jordan stood there openmouthed in surprise. Lily spent the rest of the day ignoring Jordan. Jordan felt terrible about the fight, but she was also irritated with Lily for behaving so irrationally.

Next, during her second class, Jordan unexpectedly started her period, and she had to go through the embarrassment of asking Mr. Collins for a hall pass to go to the bathroom. *At least getting my period explains my Mount Everest–sized pimple*, Jordan thought with perverse satisfaction. Even that momentary gratification disappeared when she had to borrow a pad from Michelle, the worst gossip in school.

TALK ABOUT IT

= What has been your most embarrassing school experience? How did you deal with it?

= Why do you think some people are so concerned with their appearance? Does it matter if someone has acne that he or she can't hide?

By lunchtime, everyone knew the reason why Jordan had a sweater tied around her waist.

Then, during sixth period, Jordan realized that she hadn't planned enough time for her world history project that was due on Friday. She hadn't worked on it last week at all, figuring she could cram in a few late nights this week, but she had forgotten all the extra tables and charts she had to include. Plus, she hadn't

taken into account that her teacher would keep assigning regular homework on top of the project. And she hadn't expected the essay that her English teacher just assigned for Thursday. It was going to be another week of late nights.

***

When she finally got home, she immediately walked into a fight with her mom about the disastrous state of her room. Jordan didn't understand what the big deal was. So what if she had cookie crumbs and empty soda cans on her floor? Yes, she had told her mom she would pick up, but what was the hurry? "Besides," she asked her mom, "why should I make my bed when I'm just going to mess it up again by sleeping in it?" This seemed like a perfectly reasonable point to Jordan, but her mom did not take it well.

TALK ABOUT IT

= Jordan thought she had enough time to work on her world history project, but her plans didn't account for several important factors. In your opinion, how do your planning skills compare to Jordan's? How might Jordan do better the next time?

When she finally got home, she immediately walked into a fight with her mom about the disastrous state of her room.

By the time Jordan felt up to facing her homework, she was so tired and worn out that she could barely think.

"What is going on with you?" Jordan's mom shouted at her. "I swear, some days it seems like you've been taken over by an alien!"

Jordan said something very rude, and then went to her room and slammed the door. She threw herself on her bed, stuck her head under her pillow, and screamed as loud as she could. Her anger turned to tears. Jordan's emotions were all over the place. "Maybe my mom's right," she muttered to herself. "Maybe I have been taken over by an alien."

By the time Jordan felt up to facing her homework, she was so tired and worn out that she could barely think. And she still had that project hanging over her head.

ASK THE

EXPERT

Adolescence is a time when everything about your life is changing, inside and out. Starting around age 12, your brain begins a process called remodeling. That means certain connections and pathways in your brain are forming and strengthening while others are shrinking. As your brain's frontal cortex and new connections form, you'll become better at abstract and complex thinking, critical reasoning, and seeing different perspectives. When you're under stress, the ability to go beyond the surface might not feel so great.

Meanwhile, the part of your brain called the prefrontal cortex is shrinking. That means you're not as good at thinking rationally or using logic to make decisions as you will be later. Skills like planning, impulse control, and thinking ahead aren't the strongest in your teen years. These parts of your brain won't be fully developed until your mid-twenties!

Added to your brain changes are all the changes your body is experiencing. A little before you hit puberty, your hormones go crazy. These hormonal changes may continue to affect you throughout your teen years. And your hormones affect your emotions. Being aware of these changes can help you manage them.

GET HEALTHY

- Go easy on yourself! When your life and emotions feel out of control, remind yourself that your brain and hormones are doing weird things. Someday they'll stop, and you'll feel normal again.

- Get into a good sleep routine. Teens need 8.5 to 9 hours of sleep every night. Being sleep deprived can cause a ton of issues, including extra stress and problems with learning, memory, listening, and problem-solving; acne and other skin conditions; poor behavior; unhealthy eating and weight; and overuse of caffeine or nicotine.

- Learn from your weaknesses. For example, now that Jordan knows she has trouble planning ahead for her assignments, she could schedule extra homework time during the week something is due.

THE LAST WORD FROM CARRIE

Listen to the adults you trust. They can help you make good choices, stay safe, and build healthy relationships. When you have your worst days, remind yourself that adolescence has an expiration date! If you can remember that this is just a temporary phase and implement practical survival strategies, you'll be able to enjoy and appreciate this unique time in your life.

CHAPTER TWO

TOO MANY DECISIONS

Teenagers face a lot of decisions, especially when it comes to preparing for college and careers. This process starts as early as sixth or seventh grade. Would it be better to take Spanish, French, or Mandarin? Will you take one or more of the big standardized tests? What kinds of volunteer activities will you join? Will you go to college, and which colleges would you like to attend? All of these choices have the potential to affect your future, including your career, your earnings, and the kind of person you become. Each choice can seem like the first domino in a chain reaction—tip one over and the rest of them fall down. For example, if you choose pre-algebra instead of basic math in seventh grade, by senior year you could be taking advanced placement (AP) calculus. AP classes could potentially get you into a better college, which might lead to a better job. But what if you don't take pre-algebra? Could your entire future be ruined?

Amaya found herself facing these kinds of fears. She and her friends felt a lot of pressure to make decisions that would affect the rest of their lives.

AMAYA'S STORY

Amaya was about to lose her mind. Who knew second semester of sophomore year could be so stressful? Amaya and her classmates were all taking a homeroom class called "Life GPS: Making a Map for College and Career." Their college prep counselor, Mr. Montoya, or Mr. M., was trying to help them think about their futures. Amaya knew he meant well and that it was important to plan ahead, but she thought her brain was going to explode with all the decisions she needed to make.

***

At lunch that day, she complained to her friends Kathryn and Finn. "Mr. M. says we need to have a college and career road map, and that means we need to have a destination in mind. Our future life and career goals are supposed to help us choose our

Amaya was about to lose her mind. Who knew second semester of sophomore year could be so stressful?

classes and activities now. But how am I supposed to know what career I want ten years from now? I can't even decide what I want for lunch!"

"I know, right?" said Finn. "I'm even stressed out trying to decide which product to put in my hair every morning. And now I need to choose whether I'm going to be on a pre-med, business, arts, or general track next year? Plus, I need to think about which clubs to

TALK ABOUT IT

= What is your definition of success? How is it the same as or different from the definitions that come from your parents, teachers, and peers?

= What dreams or desires do you have for your future? What kinds of plans have you made to achieve them so far?

= When you think about college and career, what kinds of thoughts and emotions come up?

= How do you approach decisions? Do you rely more on logic or instincts?

- Kathryn feels uncertain of her identity—who she is inside—not just her goals. Do you ever feel this way? If so, what is that like?

- Who would you say you are? What kinds of positive words would you use to describe yourself? What kinds of positive words would others use to describe you?

- As you gather these descriptions, what stands out to you?

- When do you feel most like yourself—the most at home in your own skin?

"I don't even know who I am now, much less who I want to be years from now!"

join that will look best on my college application!"

By now, the three friends had picked up their food from the cafeteria and were headed for the spot where they ate every day. They sat down, grabbed their food, and talked between bites.

Kathryn chimed in. "Mr. M. and my parents say that it's really important to set goals now so I can decide what colleges might be best for the major I want. That way, I can look at their requirements and make sure my courses and extracurricular activities meet or exceed them. But honestly, I don't even know who I am now, much less who I want to be years from now!"

"Same!" said Amaya. "And we're getting total mixed messages from all the adults.

First, they tell us that we have to have a long-term plan. I mean, look at all these forms and worksheets we have to fill out! *Choosing a Major. Which College Admissions Test Is Right for You? Getting into a Top-Tier University.* That last one is so confusing, it looks like a secret nuclear launch code."

"So confusing," agreed Kathryn. "Everyone says to be prepared and have specific goals in mind. But then, those very same people tell us things like, 'Don't worry. You can always change your mind. People nowadays change careers every few years anyway. And if you don't choose the right undergraduate program, there's always grad school!'" She rolled her eyes.

"So which is it?" Finn asked. "Plan like crazy or just relax because it's all going to change anyway? Our decisions are the most important we'll ever make, but they're also not? What is wrong with these people?"

"Everyone says to be prepared and have specific goals in mind. But then, those very same people tell us things like, 'Don't worry. You can always change your mind.'"

"I know!" Amaya threw up her hands. "They're torturing us with choices! It makes me want to just give up and get high."

Finn and Kathryn joined her laughter. Amaya had never used drugs, and she didn't think her friends had either, but sometimes she could see why some of her classmates chose to zone out. She poked the glop masquerading as lettuce with her plastic fork and sighed before shoving the whole tray away from her and getting up to leave.

"I'm so over this. Anyway, I need to review my notes for our biology test. I have to get at least a B+ if I want to keep my average up. I need to get an academic scholarship."

TALK ABOUT IT

= Do you ever feel like adults are giving you confusing messages about the future? If so, what do you wish they would do or say instead?

= Have you ever been tempted to use drugs or alcohol to "zone out?" What kinds of things trigger your desire to withdraw?

= What are some ways you currently cope with stress about your future and decision-making? How healthy do you think your coping methods are and why do you think so?

ASK THE

EXPERT

Amaya found planning for her future extremely stressful. She felt external pressure coming from important adults in her life—her school counselor and her parents—but also pressure from herself. She wanted to succeed, but she didn't know what success would look like to her future self. And the adults unwittingly sent her confusing signals about how to best get ready for her future, whether to map out every step or to relax and let things unfold in time.

The truth is, you need a balance between planning ahead and responding to change. Planning helps you prepare for the future to the best of your ability. But flexibility is also important, because no one can fully predict the future.

Amaya's difficulties defining her precise goals while less than halfway through high school are perfectly natural. Knowing that, perhaps you can give yourself a break when it comes to planning your future.

GET **HEALTHY**

- Talk to adults about their career and life paths. You might be surprised to find how many of them have had twists and turns along the way.

- Instead of numbing your stress in unhealthy ways, get some exercise. Physical activity produces endorphins. These feel-good chemicals in your brain give you a natural high, relieve stress, and boost your mood.

- Feeling anxiety over a high-stakes test? The biggest thing you can do to fight anxiety is to be prepared. Start studying well in advance and maintain healthy eating and sleep habits. If you find taking tests to be impossibly stressful, a counselor can offer you professional help.

THE LAST WORD FROM **CARRIE**

You can't avoid making big decisions, but you can make the process easier on yourself by treating yourself with respect and kindness. Pay attention to and honor your health, emotions, and the good things that make you special. Also, be patient with yourself! You're still growing and developing, so it makes sense that your decisions will change, too. As long as you're doing your best to make good choices and learn more about yourself along the way, you'll be just fine.

CHAPTER THREE

DRAMA QUEEN

Have you ever had stage fright, frozen up before asking someone on a date, or felt like throwing up right before a big race? We all have to face uncomfortable situations—times when we don't feel as confident as we would like. These could be anything from confronting a friend who's been talking about you behind your back, preparing to take a big test, or seeing your worst enemy headed your way when you least expect it.

When you enter adolescence, your brain undergoes developmental changes that make it very sensitive to picking up threats. Not necessarily "being chased by a lion" kinds of threats—although your brain would obviously notice those too—but more subtle dangers to your peace of mind and emotional equilibrium. Threats like catty alpha girls, sightings of your crush, grade-defining exams, and the possibility of public failure at auditions, team tryouts, or sports competitions. Your brain notices these threats and responds by sending your body into a flight, fright, or fight state. That's when you start to feel all those weird, panicky sensations in your chest or stomach.

The good news is that there are ways to calm your brain and body. Destiny experienced this flight, fright, or fight response when she auditioned for the school play.

DESTINY'S STORY

Destiny's pulse was pounding. Her lungs felt like they were about to explode. Her hands and feet felt cold and clammy, yet somehow she was sweating heavily. Her stomach was churning, and her entire body was trembling. She was convinced that the next five minutes were going to be a disaster of epic proportions.

"Come on, Destiny!" she told herself sternly, "Get yourself together. It's not like you're being chased by a hungry alligator or about to bungee jump off the Grand Canyon. All you have to do is one simple thing—pretend to be madly in love with a half-man, half-mule. Then you can go home and binge-watch whatever's on TV. Everything's going to be great!"

It was a good pep talk. Too bad Destiny didn't believe a word she'd said to herself.

Destiny was about to audition for her dream role in the school play—Queen Titania in Shakespeare's *A Midsummer Night's Dream*. She had to recite the lines from the scenes where Queen Titania, put under a spell

Destiny was about to audition for her dream role in the school play.

= **Getting the lead in the play was Destiny's dream. Do you have any dreams for your high school years? What are they?**

= **How have your dreams changed over the years? What do you think those changing dreams might reveal about the person you're becoming?**

= **Have you ever had to deal with disappointment about your dreams? Either you didn't achieve a dream—or you did, and it wasn't what you expected. What was that like?**

by her husband, Oberon, thinks she has fallen in love with a man who has the head of a donkey. Destiny knew she was born to play the part, and she'd been practicing for weeks. But as she stood behind the curtain waiting her turn, she was suddenly afraid she was going to faint.

***

Fortunately, Destiny had prepared for this moment by more than just memorizing her lines. All the younger drama students had been paired with a senior mentor. Destiny's mentor, Ava, had coached her about her stage fright. "Basically," Ava said, "when you're afraid, even if you're not in physical danger, your body and mind respond as if you are. Your heartbeat accelerates, you feel sick and shaky, and blood rushes from your head to your arms and legs. Your body is getting you ready to run away from the danger."

"Great," joked Destiny. "Maybe I should try out for the track team instead of the play."

Ava laughed. "You could do that. Or, you could use my breathing and relaxation trick. It will help your mind and body realize you're not in any danger. Everything will calm down, and you'll feel like you're in control again."

As Destiny waited backstage, she used the exercise Ava had shown her. Instead of focusing on her fear, she focused on her breathing. She closed her eyes and inhaled and exhaled slowly and deliberately, finding a comfortable pace. When her breathing was regular and rhythmic, she then concentrated on relaxing each muscle in her body, starting with her jaw and neck and moving all the way down to her toes. Gradually, as Destiny's breathing slowed and her muscles loosened, she felt her fear recede. Little by little, she began to feel calmer, steadier, and more confident.

"You could use my breathing and relaxation trick. It will help your mind and body realize you're not in any danger."

TALK ABOUT IT

= What calming strategies have you used when you've experienced fright, flight, or fight types of responses? How successful have they been?

= When do you feel calmest and most confident in yourself and your abilities?

= Do you have any mentors who can help you prepare for your next challenge? If not, is there someone you might be able to ask?

After a few minutes, Destiny opened her eyes and breathed in and out a few more times. She felt focused, alert, and peaceful. Keeping the same, slow rhythm of her breathing, she began reciting her lines to herself. She imagined herself enthralled by angelic music that had been magically conjured from a donkey's obnoxious bray.

Straightening her shoulders and holding her head high, Destiny envisioned herself as Queen Titania—tall, strong, beautiful, and utterly deluded about the object of her affection. "Been there, done that," she thought to herself wryly, before slipping back into character. When the play's director called her name, she was ready.

Straightening her shoulders and holding her head high, Destiny envisioned herself as Queen Titania—tall, strong, beautiful.

TALK ABOUT IT

▪ Is there a character from literature, film, television, or the arts that you admire and want to be like? What about this person appeals to you? What steps can you take to model yourself after him or her?

▪ Think of a time when you've successfully faced a challenge or achieved a goal. What did you learn about yourself? What can you take away for next time?

ASK THE
EXPERT

Destiny's stage fright is one example of the flight, fright, or fight response that your body might have in reaction to stress. When you're in a situation that seems difficult or uncomfortable, your body and brain both react. Heart and breathing rates increase, blood flows to the muscles in your arms and legs, your feet and hands feel cold and clammy, your stomach churns, and you feel anxious.

The good news is that the same processes in your body that turn on a stress response can also turn it off. The body's answer to the stress response is the relaxation response. When your body and mind no longer feel threatened, your heart rate and breathing return to a normal rate. Your muscles and stomach relax. Your emotions equalize.

The breathing and relaxation technique Ava taught Destiny is one way to set your body's relaxation response in motion. Paying attention to and slowing your breathing convinces your body that it isn't in any danger. As your stress and anxiety recede, you'll be able to focus on what you need to do. Whether you're aiming to be queen of the stage or queen of the world, you'll be poised to conquer your fears and achieve your goals.

GET **HEALTHY**

- Destiny's breathing exercise comes in many versions. You can try hers or find others online when you need some help facing fears or calming down.

- Rehearsing isn't just for plays! If you know you're going to face a stressful situation, practice what you're going to do ahead of time.

- Confront your fears gradually and in small doses. For example, if you're a nervous driver, you could practice driving to a nearby store and then work up to longer distances as you get more comfortable.

- Use the power of peer pressure for good! Get a group of friends to join you in an activity that scares you. When you see them having fun, you'll be more likely to get involved than you would on your own.

THE LAST WORD FROM **CARRIE**

As you mature and gain more experience, you'll develop different ways to evaluate and respond to people and situations your brain perceives as threats. Your teenage brain is more plastic, or able to change, than an adult brain. It's important to deal with stress in a positive way, because changes you make in your brain as an adolescent will stick around when you're an adult. Like Destiny, you can learn to face your fears like you're royalty.

CHAPTER FOUR

PRACTICALLY PERFECT

When you become a teenager, it can seem like everyone is always expecting things from you. Your parents want you to do well in school, keep up with your chores, and keep your little brother out of trouble. Your coach is always yelling that he expects "one thousand percent!" at swim practice. Your teachers all expect you to prioritize their assignments as though you didn't have six other teachers throwing homework at you. Your friends want you to follow their social media posts and keep up with the latest trends, and your best friend expects you to make time for just the two of you. Your art teacher returns your line drawings if you don't use exactly the right kind of charcoal pencil. Meanwhile, you might hear this voice inside your head that won't shut up. It says things like:

"Justina's always going to be a faster swimmer than you."

"Why did you miss that note during the choral performance? You ruined the whole thing."

"Sophie is so beautiful. Why can't you have a body like hers?"

"You haven't studied enough for your test. Your teacher is going to know you're unprepared."

Sound familiar? Trina often said similar things to herself. She had felt pressure to be perfect almost her whole life, but lately everything was piling up on her. How can she find a way to stop comparing herself to other people and learn to be OK with imperfection?

TRINA'S STORY

"I'm so jealous of you, Trina," moaned Asha. "I wish I was as perfectly put together as you are."

"Me, too," added Kurt as the group walked out of school together. "You make everything look so easy."

"Me, three," added Mei, not to be outdone. "I can't believe how good you are at everything you do. I can barely survive school by itself, and you've got ballet, violin, debate club, and a 4.0 average."

"It's only a 3.93 average," protested Trina. "Remember? I got an A- in Trig last semester."

"Oh. No." said Mei, enunciating each word in mock horror. "There goes your chance to get into Harvard."

Everyone laughed at Mei's joke, including Trina. But inside, Trina wasn't so certain Mei was wrong. She was far from perfect! It wasn't just her math grade. It was also her freckles. She

wished she had Mei's perfectly smooth, clear skin and Kurt's long eyelashes. And even though Asha was so clumsy she could barely walk without crashing into something, Trina envied her elegant-looking hands and feet. Trina looked dolefully down at her shoes, which were currently covering the crooked pinky toes she despised. If only those toes were straight, she knew she would be a better dancer.

TALK ABOUT IT

= **Do you ever feel like others see you differently than you see yourself? What do you think people misunderstand about you? What do you wish they knew?**

= **What kinds of things do you say to yourself when you compare yourself to other people? How does that make you feel?**

***

To any outsider, Trina looked confident and calm. But inside, she was a mess. Every day, she made a mental list of all her flaws, mistakes, and ways she failed to measure up to her expectations. The list never seemed to get any shorter, no matter how hard she tried.

To any outsider, Trina looked confident and calm. But inside, she was a mess.

Trina brought the same energy to her schoolwork. She obsessed over all her assignments—rewriting, correcting, and rewriting again. Yet she was always nervous

when she turned something in, because she just knew there was something important that she missed. She was certain her teacher was going to find something wrong. The fact that her

= Do you consider yourself a perfectionist? Why or why not?

= Do you recognize any of Trina's thoughts and worries from your own life? Which ones? What other worries do you have, if any?

= Have you ever visited the planet of Self-Pity? What's that like? When are you most likely to visit it? The least likely?

Mei broke into Trina's dark thoughts. "Earth to Trina," she said, giving her a poke. "What planet are you on?"

teachers almost never found anything wrong didn't alter Trina's convictions in the least.

***

Mei broke into Trina's dark thoughts. "Earth to Trina," she said, giving her a poke. "What planet are you on?"

"The planet of Self-Pity," muttered Trina. "I was just thinking of our book report due next week. I don't totally understand the symbolism in *Of Mice and Men*. I just know I'm gonna blow it."

Mei looked at her sideways. "You know you're not going to do any such thing, right?"

When Trina didn't respond right away, Mei poked her again, harder this time. "Right?"

"OK! I guess so!" Trina conceded. "But . . ."

"Let me take over from here," Asha butted in. She got

right in Trina's face, looked directly into her eyes, and grabbed her head between her hands. "Repeat after me: 'I am Trina the Destroyer. I am a John Steinbeck *monster*. I will crush this report. I will blow this report to smithereens, pick up the pieces, and stomp on them!'"

"Don't forget, 'and light them on fire!'" chirped Mei.

"I'm not going to say that!" protested Trina. "That's the dumbest thing ever!"

"Quiet!" Asha barked. "Just do what you're told."

"Yes, Mom," grumbled Trina. She took a deep breath, trying not to laugh at the ridiculousness of it all.

"I am Trina the Destroyer," she began, gaining confidence and volume as she went.

Before she got to the end of her first sentence, all three of her friends were snickering. By the time she got past "smithereens" and to "light them on fire," they were clutching their stomachs. Even Trina was snorting with laughter.

"Whew," said Kurt, wiping his eyes on his sleeve. "I don't know about you, Trina, but I feel better."

"Me, too," said Trina with surprise.

TALK ABOUT IT

- Do you have any worries that you know deep down are unrealistic? What do you suppose keeps you from letting them go? What do you think might help you get rid of them?

- Laughter really is the best medicine! What kinds of things make you laugh even when you're feeling bad about yourself?

- Trina's friends helped her to cope in a positive way with her perfectionism. What kinds of things do your friends say and do that are helpful to you?

- Although she didn't use this terminology, Asha helped Trina practice self-affirmation, which is making positive declarations about yourself designed to create change. Self-affirmations help you feel better about yourself, reduce stress, and accept that mistakes do happen. Is this something you'd be willing to try? Why or why not?

ASK THE
EXPERT

Perfectionists like Trina are good at almost everything they do. But one secret to their success is that they are so afraid of failure that they rarely try something new if they don't already know they'll be great at it. Perfectionists often feel like they will never be good enough or look good enough. Many hear a constant voice in their heads telling them that one mistake could ruin everything. That's why many perfectionists are also procrastinators, because if they don't start something, they're guaranteed not to mess it up!

What all perfectionists need to learn is that no one is perfect. In fact, if you see someone who seems perfect, chances are that he or she feels just as confused and anxious on the inside as you do. To get past all this anxiety, perfectionists have to learn to accept and embrace things that are less than perfect. Reformed perfectionists still set goals and challenges for themselves, but they don't beat themselves up if they don't achieve them. They're able to let things go because their sense of self isn't dependent on being perfect and getting everything right. Instead, they are able to have fun in the moment, take risks, and see mistakes and failures as opportunities to grow and learn.

GET **HEALTHY**

- To banish perfectionism, practice imperfection. Start making small mistakes on purpose and evaluate the results.

- When you're facing a challenge, focus on your abilities, not your weaknesses. For example, you could say to yourself, "Even though this assignment is really hard, what are some ways that it's going well?"

- Practice self-compassion. Self-compassion includes mindfulness, being as kind and caring to yourself as you would be to a friend, and reminding yourself you're not the only one who feels the way you do. Self-compassion relieves stress and feelings of isolation.

- Don't be afraid to ask for professional help. You don't need to suffer with your perfectionism alone!

THE LAST WORD FROM **CARRIE**

Perfectionism can have its rewards. But the downside of perfectionism is that you never truly get to enjoy any of it because you're too busy being self-critical and afraid.

Instead of aiming for an impossible perfection and engaging in critical self-talk, practice being as kind and compassionate to yourself as you are to your best friends. Celebrate all the good things you are and do, while keeping the not-so-good stuff in perspective and appreciating the lessons you've learned as a result. And practice messing up once in a while! You might be surprised how much fun it can be. Maybe you won't quite learn to love your imperfections, but you can make friends with them—and in the process, make friends with your wonderfully imperfect self.

CHAPTER FIVE

FAMILY FAILS

Whether you have one parent, two parents, or more; an adopted family or a stepfamily; a nuclear family or an extended one; your family is a big part of your life and identity. Regardless of what is going on in your life, ideally you can count on your family to be there—even if that means your little sister consistently leaves a mess in your room or your dad makes incredibly embarrassing jokes when your date comes to pick you up.

But what if suddenly you couldn't count on your family to be there in quite the same way? Changes in our families can throw us out of our safe, familiar routines and cause a lot of stress. This is especially true with unexpected or unwanted changes, such as incarceration, a death, or someone in the family facing severe medical, physical, or emotional problems. But even expected and exciting changes, like the birth or adoption of a new baby or a parent getting a new job, can cause disruption and confusion as everyone adjusts to new circumstances or even a new way of life.

Mika's life was upended when her parents separated. Suddenly the happy family she was used to didn't exist anymore. She wondered whether she would ever recognize her own life again.

MIKA'S STORY

Mika didn't know exactly when it all started, but looking back, she could see that her parents had been acting strangely for at least a year. It wasn't obvious at first, but now that Mika reflected on it, her mom and dad had stopped touching each other. They used to be an affectionate couple, kissing and embracing often.

Mika hadn't consciously noticed when that changed. Otherwise she might have realized what was coming. Two weeks ago, her mom and dad gathered Mika and her brother Zach together for a family conference and dropped the bombshell. They were getting a divorce.

Mika was devastated. But there was worse news to come. "Kids," said their dad carefully. "I'm really sorry, but I'm going to start a new job in a different state. I'll be moving at the end of

Mika was devastated. But there was worse news to come.

the month. I know it's going to be a big change, but I want you to know I'm always going to be there for you both."

Mika didn't know what she was supposed to say to that. All of a sudden, nothing in her life seemed to make sense. It was like an earthquake had rumbled through her family and she was watching it collapse around her.

***

Their parents both wanted to talk more to Mika and Zach, but Mika rebuffed their efforts at communication. She stormed off to bed and tossed and turned all night. For the next two weeks, she avoided her parents before she left for school and spent most of her time afterward studying in her room. But even though she refused to talk to her parents, she couldn't escape the emotions churning inside her like a huge storm. Home didn't

All of a sudden, nothing in her life seemed to make sense.

TALK ABOUT IT

▪ Have you ever experienced a significant change in your family, whether positive or negative? What was that like for you?

▪ What emotions do you think Mika was feeling? What emotions do you think you would feel in her place?

▪ Think of a time you didn't know what to say to your parents. What was going on inside you at the time? Why do you think you might have had trouble communicating your thoughts and feelings?

= Do you think Mika was actually angry at Taylor? Why or why not? Why do you think she lost her temper with her best friend?

= Have you ever felt like your home wasn't really your home? What caused you to feel that way?

= Do you think it was a good strategy for Mika to avoid her parents? What would you have done in her situation?

> Mika found the pressure unbearable. She had difficulty concentrating on anything at school.

feel like home anymore, and the day her dad was going to move out kept rushing closer.

Mika found the pressure unbearable. She had difficulty concentrating on anything at school. If she wasn't wrestling with insomnia, she had disturbing dreams. She even snapped at her best friend Taylor, which she didn't usually do.

***

Taylor was sympathetic. Her parents were still together, but their family had changed drastically two years ago when her younger brother Emmett had become seriously ill. Although Emmett was better now than he was before, he was still confined to bed most days.

"Do you want to talk about it, Mika?" Taylor asked.

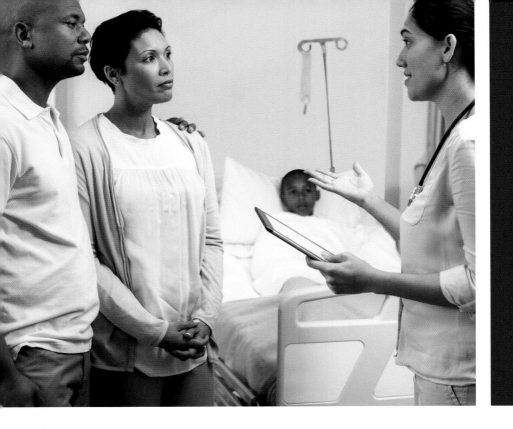

Mika didn't, but she knew she needed to. "How did you get through it when Emmett got sick?" she asked.

"It was unbelievably hard," Taylor said. "I love my brother more than anything, but I was furious at him at the same time. His sickness changed everything, even if it wasn't his fault. Mom and dad hardly seemed to have any time or attention for me. I felt lost and confused and guilty for feeling so miserable when it was my brother who was suffering—all these crazy emotions at once."

"I feel some of those emotions, too, even though my situation isn't the same," said Mika quietly. "It helps to know that. Maybe I'm not as insane as I've been feeling."

"You're definitely not," Taylor assured her.

"When did it get better for you?" asked Mika.

Taylor thought for several seconds, then shrugged. "It took a while. I mean, Emmett is still sick and that's hard, but it's somehow become more normal. I got used to it, and I know that going through it has made me stronger.

"Not just mentally stronger, either," Taylor boasted. "I've had to help so much with lifting Emmett that I have killer biceps. Look at this muscle definition!"

Mika shook her head at her friend, but she felt the corner of her mouth quirking up. "I don't know if I'm going to get any arm muscles out of this divorce," she said thoughtfully, "but I suppose I can hang on for my new normal, too."

"I feel some of those emotions, too, even though my situation isn't the same," said Mika.

TALK ABOUT IT

▪ Do you have a friend you can talk to about important or difficult things in your life? What qualities make him or her a good person to turn to for support?

▪ Taylor was able to encourage Mika and reassure her she wasn't going crazy. Is there anything else you would say to Mika if you could?

▪ When in your life have you had to adjust to a big change? What was that process like? How did you grow as a result?

ASK THE

EXPERT

Any significant change in a family can be a source of stress, even if it's a joyful change, like a new baby. When it's a change you didn't want, like an illness or a divorce, stress is even more likely. When that happens, it's helpful to have someone outside of your family to confide in. Mika's confidant of choice was her best friend, Taylor. Because Taylor had already been through a drastic, stressful change in her own family, she could empathize and offer perspective to Mika. Taylor was also a good listener, not forcing Mika to talk but being available when Mika was ready to do so. She didn't judge Mika for her feelings but instead offered empathy and reassurance. Finally, Taylor didn't try to give Mika perfect answers or quick fixes. She acknowledged that adjusting to change takes time and that things might not return to the way they were before.

If changes in your family are causing you stress, take a cue from Mika and share your feelings with a person you trust. Pick someone whom you know is a nonjudgmental, empathetic listener. In addition to a good friend, you can reach out to a sibling who is old enough to understand and support you, a relative, a mentor, or someone else whose wisdom and discretion you trust.

GET HEALTHY

- Even if you're feeling miserable, do your best to eat and sleep well, exercise, and do things that you enjoy.

- Get some nature therapy! Being outside and moving your body, especially in the sunshine, is a great way to relieve stress.

- Give yourself time. Whether the change in your family happened overnight or over a long period of time, you will need a while to get used to it. Instead of berating yourself for your feelings, assure yourself that you will adjust eventually.

- Find ways to focus on the positive, even if only in small ways, like Taylor did with her stronger arms. Be proud that this experience will make you a stronger person.

THE LAST WORD FROM CARRIE

Whatever shape or configuration your family comes in, it can be your rock or it can be the epicenter of your own personal earthquake. When the people you count on to always be there for you suddenly aren't there, or aren't there in the same way, it can be a shocking and disorienting experience. Whether your family quake is a tiny temblor like your older sister leaving for college, a catastrophic upheaval like a death, or something in between like a new stepfamily, you'll maintain your sanity best if you can keep yourself grounded despite the tremors. Even when you feel like doing anything but taking care of yourself, make your best effort to exercise, eat right, get enough sleep, enjoy nature, and turn to your friends for support. Above all, know that you will come through this stressful time a stronger, wiser, and more experienced person.

CHAPTER SIX

PROBLEM FRIENDS

P art of being a good friend is supporting your friends
when they are having problems. That can mean many
things, like listening to a friend talk about his problems
or sitting quietly with him when he's too upset to speak. Or it
could mean comforting a girlfriend with her favorite treats when
a crush disappoints her.

But sometimes a friend may have issues that aren't as
simple to deal with—ones that persist for a long time or have
the potential for serious, lasting physical or emotional damage.
These kinds of problems may be beyond the ability of any
teenager to handle all alone.

Jasmine found herself so caught up in the problems of her
friends Sydney and Charlotte that they began to seem like her
problems, too. She had to learn how to deal with her friends'
struggles in a way that was healthy for her friends *and* for her.

JASMINE'S STORY

Jasmine didn't have any problems. Or to be specific, she didn't have any problems of her own. She loved being part of a Science, Technology, Engineering, and Math (STEM) school and dreamed about becoming a genetic scientist like her hero, Rosalind Franklin, who helped discover DNA. No, the problem wasn't Jasmine—it was her friends and their perpetual crisis modes. Somehow, their problems always seemed to become her responsibility.

Jasmine's friend Sydney struggled with depression and anxiety. For a few days in a row, Jasmine noticed Sydney wearing a long-sleeved hoodie, even though the heat was sweltering. Finally, she asked her about it.

Sydney claimed that she was bundled up because she wasn't feeling well. Jasmine thought that was fishy, but she let it go . . . this time. As the weather got hotter and Sydney still wore long sleeves, Jasmine's concern grew. Every few days, she'd ask Sydney whether she was OK. Finally, Sydney seemed to understand that Jasmine wasn't going to drop the subject. She pulled Jasmine

> Jasmine's friend Sydney struggled with depression and anxiety.

into an empty classroom, swallowed hard, and rolled up her sleeves. Her arms were covered with long, shallow cuts, some scabbed over and some clearly fresh.

Jasmine gasped. "Sydney, what happened?"

Sydney avoided her eye. "I've been cutting myself," she said softly. "I don't want to, but it feels like pressure keeps building up inside me. When I cut, the pressure releases a little."

"You have to get help!" Jasmine insisted. "You need to talk to the school counselor, or your mom or dad, or a doctor."

"You have to get help!" Jasmine insisted.

"No!" Sydney was distraught. "I don't want to get in trouble or burden my parents. Please, promise me you won't tell anyone."

Jasmine felt trapped. She didn't want to promise, but she didn't want to betray Sydney's trust, so she agreed to keep quiet. Yet the secret weighed on her. Her fears that Sydney might seriously harm herself prevented her from sleeping well or focusing on her schoolwork. Even a new documentary about famous women in science couldn't pique her interest. To make things worse, Jasmine's friend Charlotte was always full of drama. This time it was another so-called crisis with

her boyfriend. She kept texting Jasmine and freaking out if Jasmine didn't text back right away.

***

TALK ABOUT IT

- **Have you ever known anyone who has self-harming behaviors or was being harmed by someone else, either physically or emotionally? How did that make you feel?**

- **Have you ever had a friend like Charlotte who seems caught in crisis mode and relies on you for comfort? How do you feel about this relationship?**

- **How do you think Jasmine should respond to Charlotte's demands for attention?**

- **What are some ways that you show support to friends who are having problems?**

Between the two of them, Jasmine felt strained and frayed. She felt like her friends' problems were contagious, along with their tears, anxiety, and depression. Was it possible for a person to be an emotional vampire? Sydney was the one cutting herself, but Jasmine felt like she was bleeding too.

After a week of stress-induced stomachaches and nonstop worry, Jasmine couldn't take it anymore. She pulled Sydney aside during a break between classes. "I'm sorry," she whispered. "But I have to tell someone. I'm scared that you're going to seriously hurt yourself."

Sydney's face turned red with anger. "You can't do that!" she hissed. "I trusted you not to tell anyone!"

"I know," said Jasmine softly. "But I have to do it. I want to help you, but I just don't have the ability or the experience. You need to talk to an adult—someone who can actually help you."

"Besides," she added, still speaking in a low voice, but with more intensity, "it's not fair of you to ask me to keep this secret. You don't realize how hard it's been for me to stand by and watch you hurt yourself like this."

***

Sydney argued more but subsided when Jasmine wouldn't change her mind. She agreed that Jasmine could tell their school counselor, Ms. Gia. As soon as Jasmine talked to Ms. Gia, she felt a huge sense of relief, like an enormous boulder had been lifted off her shoulders. She was still anxious for her friend's well-being, but she trusted that Sydney would get the help she needed.

Ms. Gia also offered to help Jasmine process her own feelings of depression and stress and create healthy boundaries. Jasmine needed to be able to support friends like Sydney and Charlotte without feeling responsible for fixing their crises. Ms. Gia also reminded Jasmine to spend

TALK ABOUT IT

▪ Have you ever been so worried about a friend that you couldn't think about anything else? How did you manage your fears? What helped you regain your focus?

▪ Have you ever needed to go to an adult for help with a friend's problems? What kinds of problems do you think would cause you to ask for help?

time with friends who were emotionally stable and healthy, not just those who were struggling. Instead of always being the one who gave help, she needed to be able to rely on people who could be there for her. Jasmine felt hopeful she could get back to her old, positive self and still be helpful to her friends.

TALK ABOUT IT

= Do you think Jasmine did the right thing by telling Ms. Gia about Sydney's cutting? What would you have done?

= Do you agree that boundaries are important in friendships? Why or why not?

= Do you have friends who are emotionally healthy? How can you tell? What's it like to be around them?

Jasmine felt hopeful she could get back to her old, positive self and still be helpful to her friends.

ASK THE

EXPERT

If you're an empathetic person like Jasmine, you may take on your friends' problems and emotions as though they are your own. Of course, it's not bad to want to support your friends, but it's crucial for your own mental health to maintain good boundaries. No matter how much you may care, you are ultimately not able to prevent or take responsibility for anyone else's suffering.

An important aspect of having good boundaries—not taking the weight of the world on your shoulders—is knowing when you need to get professional assistance. When it comes to serious, potentially life-threatening situations like self-harm, severe depression, or suicidal thoughts, don't worry about what your friend will think of you if you go to an adult on their behalf. Even if they feel betrayed at first, your intervention may save their life.

Although you may feel selfish for worrying about yourself when a friend is hurting, it's crucial that you practice self-care. Finding friendships that nurture you instead of drain your energy and taking time for rest and enjoyable activities will ensure that you stay mentally and emotionally healthy. By being a good friend to yourself, you'll maintain the strength and resilience you need to be a good friend to others.

GET HEALTHY

- If one of your friends is having a crisis, try to enlist a group of friends to support them. That way, you're not the only one your friend relies on. This will be better for you both in the long run.

- Talk to a trusted adult, like a parent, a counselor, or a doctor. If your friend's problem is so severe that you're afraid his or her life may be in danger, don't wait for permission to involve an adult.

- Try to have some balance in your friendships. If all of your friends seem to be in crisis, you may need to seek out new friends who are more emotionally stable.

THE LAST WORD FROM CARRIE

Jasmine faced a serious challenge in learning how to best care for friends who weren't caring for themselves without losing herself in the process. Establishing strong boundaries and healthy friendships is crucial to your well-being. While there are many ways to support your friends, accepting responsibility for their problems and keeping dangerous secrets for them isn't good for them or for you. Understanding your friends' limits—and yours—will help you protect and maintain your mental health.

CHAPTER SEVEN

BEATING THE BLUES

Everyone feels sad or anxious some of the time, especially when something doesn't go your way—like when you have an argument with a friend, put a scratch on your dad's new car, or get the world's ugliest sweater for your birthday instead of the smartphone you wanted. But some teens find that their sadness and worry doesn't go away. They find that they can't enjoy the things that normally make them happy, whether it's listening to music, reading their favorite novels, or volunteering to tutor elementary school kids after school. They may struggle to keep up with schoolwork and extracurricular activities or spend more time sleeping, watching TV, or eating junk food than usual. Or they may not eat much at all. They may feel guilty about things that aren't their fault or be extremely fearful of things that objectively aren't that frightening.

If you know someone like this, they may be suffering from clinical anxiety or depression. These are medical conditions that require the intervention of a professional psychologist or psychiatrist.

Kiki's friends noticed she had many of these warning signs of anxiety and depression. She needed her counselor and the people who cared about her to help her to regain her zest for life.

KIKI'S STORY

"Kiki!" Kiki's teammate screamed at her as she charged down the field with the ball, but Kiki barely noticed. She should have been ready to receive the pass. Instead, she hit the ground as a defender from the Buxton Panthers plowed into her.

Kiki was vaguely aware of the shrill burst of a whistle and her coach yelling at the referee. She thought her shin and ankle were bruised, but she couldn't bring herself to care. Typically, Kiki would have been infuriated with the other player. Today when the game ended, she wasn't even sure whether her team had won or lost.

Kiki was normally an outgoing, aggressive forward on her soccer team, but recently her skills had been slipping. She was distracted and lethargic and losing the toned muscles she once took pride in. Sometimes she didn't bother showing up for practice at all. Once she missed a match, and Coach Garrison was livid.

Off the field, things weren't any better. Instead of hanging out with her team, Kiki stayed at home. When her teammates showed

■ Have you ever been injured while playing a sport or doing some kind of physical activity? What happened? How did you respond?

■ Have you ever felt disconnected from yourself, other people, and things going on around you? What was that like for you? What do you think led to that feeling?

■ Do you recognize any of Kiki's other symptoms in yourself or in others?

up at her house or called, she always seemed to be sleeping or mindlessly watching TV. When she did talk to them, she made morbid jokes about death and dying. She finally confessed that sometimes just thinking about having to face another practice or game made her feel like she was choking.

***

After hearing from multiple team members that they were concerned about her, Coach Garrison went to Kiki's parents.

Her parents then asked Kiki what was going on. She gave them nearly emotionless answers. "Everything's too hard and scary," she said. "I don't see the point of trying."

Worried about her uncharacteristic sadness, Kiki's parents sent her to a counselor who specialized in working with adolescents. Dr. Rosa welcomed Kiki into a private room with a

"Everything's too hard and scary," she said. "I don't see the point of trying."

comfortable sofa. She had a calm, warm manner that put Kiki at
ease. Dr. Rosa asked Kiki to tell her a little about herself and then
followed up with some questions about how Kiki was feeling. "I
feel pretty terrible," Kiki admitted. "I feel hopeless all the time.
I've started hating soccer and I don't understand why. Even

After a few more questions, Dr. Rosa asked Kiki whether she had ever had suicidal thoughts.

TALK ABOUT IT

- Have you ever thought that death might come as a relief? What do you think caused you to feel that way? What, if anything, helped that feeling to go away?

- If you still feel this way, have you considered getting help? What steps might you take in order to get the help you need?

thinking about lacing on my cleats makes me feel sick."

After a few more questions, Dr. Rosa asked Kiki whether she had ever had suicidal thoughts. Kiki admitted that she thought about death constantly. "I don't plan to kill myself or anything," she said tonelessly, "but dying seems like it would be a relief."

After talking with Kiki a little longer, Dr. Rosa told Kiki, "From what you've said to me, it sounds like you are experiencing anxiety and depression." When Kiki looked blank, Dr. Rosa elaborated, "Everyone feels a certain amount of worry, fear, or nervousness as they go through life. And everyone experiences sadness and times of low energy or interest. But when those feelings are prolonged and interfere with your ability to live your life, then we begin to see them as symptoms of treatable medical conditions called anxiety and depression.

"They're not the same condition, but it's quite common for teens to have both," Dr. Rosa added, "perhaps because anxiety can lead to depression."

***

Dr. Rosa explained to Kiki that her treatment would consist of cognitive behavioral therapy (CBT). "CBT will teach you how to recognize negative thinking patterns about yourself, others, the things that are happening to you, and the future," she told Kiki. "Once you recognize those patterns, you'll be able to challenge and change them. We can also talk about the sources of your anxiety about soccer and why your feelings toward it have shifted so drastically. Once you identify the experiences or fears at the root of your anxiety, CBT will also help you gradually face and overcome them."

TALK ABOUT IT

= Do you know anyone who has seen a therapist for depression, anxiety, or something else? What was their reason for going?

= Have you ever seen or considered seeing a therapist? Why or why not?

"CBT will teach you how to recognize negative thinking patterns about yourself."

Kiki thought CBT sounded about as fun as blocking a goal shot with her face. But gradually, through CBT and with the help of Dr. Rosa, she began feeling more in control of her fears as she taught herself to think in more positive ways. For example, when she caught herself thinking that everything was too hard, she stopped and told herself, "That's an untrue generalization.

What's a more accurate way to think about my life?" As the lessons from CBT sunk in and with Dr. Rosa's support, Kiki resumed her social and athletic activities. The sickening knot of fear in her stomach when she thought about soccer began to ease.

After six months of therapy, Kiki's depression and anxiety were under control, and she was nearly back to peak physical condition. Soccer season was over, but Kiki was already looking forward to next year.

"I feel like I'm awake and alive again," she told her teammates one day when they gathered for an off-season pizza party. "It's going to be a great season next year," she added as they all traded high fives. "The next time we play them, those Panthers are going *down*."

TALK ABOUT IT

= Do you have any negative thinking patterns that you would like to change? What are they and when do they usually show up?

= What is one negative thought pattern that you would like to question or challenge? In what ways might you be thinking something inaccurate or untrue about something or someone in your life?

= What fears do you experience on a regular basis? How do you typically deal with them?

= Can you remember when a particular fear began? If so, what was going on in your life or in your thoughts when you first noticed it?

ASK THE

EXPERT

Teenage girls are at a higher risk for anxiety and depression than boys. That makes it extra important for girls to be aware of the symptoms of both. Kiki experienced depression and anxiety together, but it's also possible to have anxiety without depression, or, more rarely, depression without anxiety. Potential signs of clinical anxiety include significant distress, extreme behavior changes, and impaired function at school. Other signs are increased social isolation, trouble bouncing back from minor setbacks, fears that seem out of proportion, and worry that seems unusually severe.

No one knows exactly what causes depression, but one possibility is low levels of serotonin, a neurotransmitter that helps send messages in the brain. That's why antidepressant medications often increase serotonin levels. Other possible contributors to depression are structural abnormalities in the brain, genetics, the environment, and stress.

CBT also produces changes in your brain—good ones! Because the adolescent brain is still forming until around age 25, learning new, healthier thought patterns can produce long-lasting physical alterations in the brain. This is great news! It means that with help, teens may be able to retrain their brains to "grow out of" anxiety and depression.

GET **HEALTHY**

- Get moving! For some people, regular exercise can be as effective for depression as medication or therapy.

- Challenge negative thinking by asking yourself, "What is the evidence for and against this thought?" "Are there reasons my worries might not be true?" "Is there another way to look at my situation?"

- Hormonal fluctuations might cause you to feel more depressed before your period. Thankfully, this usually will pass once your period starts. Vitamin B-6 may help with PMS-related symptoms.

THE LAST WORD FROM **CARRIE**

Kiki was fortunate to have caring teammates who noticed she wasn't her normal self and intervened to get her help. If you suspect you may have depression or anxiety, you can also get help. A therapist can determine whether you are clinically anxious or depressed and a psychiatrist can determine whether you need antidepressant medications. They can get you started on CBT, supplements, or other treatment options, as well as help you establish healthy eating, sleep, and exercise habits.

Kiki felt better after six months of therapy, but other people might need more treatment to see a difference. That's OK. It's also OK to return to therapy if you find yourself falling into old fears and negative thought patterns. The goal is not to leave therapy behind forever, but to have it in your toolbox if and when you need a little assistance beating back those blues.

CHAPTER EIGHT

SLEEPOVER

This probably isn't news to you, but teens think and talk a lot about sex! Who is doing it, who wants to do it, who's never done it, who is maybe doing too much of it. Of all the pressures of being a teenager, pressure to have sex may be the toughest one to manage, especially when it can seem like everyone else is having it. But a lot of this is talk only. In 2017, only 40 percent of all high school students have ever had sex.

Some of the talk is nothing more than juicy gossip, but often what people think and choose to do about sex reflects deeper values about love, relationships, bodies, religion, or identity. And when you're in a relationship—or even when you're not—you might feel pressure to act sexually in a way that's not consistent with the way you think and feel or the things you believe.

Gabriella felt this pressure when her boyfriend asked her to have sex with him after a few months of dating. She cared about him, but she wasn't sure she was ready to take such a big step. She turned to her girlfriends for advice.

GABRIELLA'S STORY

"And that," Gabriella said, looking significantly at her friends, who were sprawled beside her in their pajamas, "is when Paul told me his parents were away on a business trip and asked if I would spend all day Saturday with him. So that we could, *you know*." She turned red when she said the last two words.

Luca bolted upright, nearly choking on the chip she was eating. "No way! I can't believe he asked you that!"

"I can," said Zoe, the third member of the trio, dropping the magazine she was reading. "It's that whole 'toxic masculinity' thing, you know, where guys think they have to act tough and get girls to sleep with them."

Luca frowned at her. "Maybe," she said. "But not all guys fall for that kind of pressure. And not every guy has bad motives for wanting to have sex."

"My boyfriend's pretty sensitive," admitted Zoe. She snickered. "His mom would kill him if he wasn't. Last week I was over for dinner and she gave this whole speech about how she and Jayden's dad raised her boys to be 'men who respect women and are in touch with their feelings, not misogynistic beer commercial clichés.' I think she's my new hero."

> **"I guess the first question is, what do you want to do?"**

"Can we get back to the point?" Gabriella pleaded. "I could really use some advice."

"Oh, fine," Zoe retorted. "I guess the first question is, what do you want to do?"

"If I knew that, I wouldn't be asking you for help," complained Gabriella. "I mean, I always thought I would wait until I got

= **What do you think about what Paul asked Gabriella? How would you feel if someone asked you something similar?**

= **Have you encountered any of the false beliefs and stereotypes that are part of toxic masculinity, such as, "real men don't cry," "real men are strong and aggressive," or "real men don't act like girls"? Where do you see these ideas being communicated? Do you know any teens, regardless of gender, who feel under pressure to behave certain ways because of these patterns of thinking?**

= **Where do you think your ideas about gender have come from? What problems might be caused by expecting people to limit themselves to stereotypically "masculine" or "feminine" behaviors? Can you think of people you know who aren't defined by these societal expectations?**

engaged or married or at least until I was a lot older—that's what my parents and I have talked about anyway. But now there's Paul. We've only been together two months, but I really care about him and I want us to be happy. And maybe sex is part of that."

"OK," said Zoe. "Let's back up a bit. When you and Paul are usually together—you know, when you're making out all over school and grossing us all out—how do you talk about consent?"

Gabriella blushed. "I don't know that we do talk about it."

"So how does he know that you're OK with what he's doing?" Luca asked. "Does he ask if he can kiss you? Put his arms around you? Touch you over or under your clothes?"

Gabriella turned even redder than before. "Only over the clothes so far. And he doesn't ask. He just kind of, I don't know, makes a move. And I either let him or I don't. If he can tell I'm uncomfortable, he'll back off."

"Whoa, wait a minute," demanded Zoe, sitting straight up. "That's not how consent works. He's supposed to ask you every single time whether you're OK with something *before* he does it, not just do it and wait to get stopped. And he's supposed to get verbal permission from you. Mind reading is not a real thing."

"He's supposed to get verbal permission from you. Mind reading is not a real thing."

"We did talk about consent at first," said Gabriella. "But since then, it just hasn't seemed necessary. He knows I'm OK with kissing him. Why does he need to keep asking?"

"Well, you did just say sometimes you're uncomfortable, right?" Luca was stretched out on the floor again, propping herself on her elbows. "Just because you're generally OK with kissing doesn't mean you want to every time. He shouldn't assume. Besides, it goes both ways. You're supposed to ask if he's OK with what you want to do, too."

"So we're supposed to have this conversation every single time?" Gabriella said doubtfully. "That doesn't sound very romantic to me."

Zoe raised an eyebrow. "Showing each other respect and consideration isn't romantic? But him asking you to have sneaky sex when his parents aren't home is?"

Luca's eyes shone with mischief. "Maybe he thinks you'll be so turned on by the pile of sweaty socks in his room that you'll swoon into his arms."

"Eww." Gabriella wrinkled her nose.

"I say you go for it." Luca flapped her hand in Gabriella's direction. "Besides, you know if you don't, Caitlin Williams from biology class will. She can't wait to get between his sheets."

TALK ABOUT IT

- What is your understanding of consent? How have you talked about it in the past with your friends or romantic interests? What have those conversations been like? If consent isn't something you talk about, what do you think would help you to get comfortable with that kind of discussion?

- Do you agree with Gabriella that talking about consent every single time isn't romantic? Why or why not? What are some ways you could help to make it feel romantic to you and your partner?

- Other than from your friends, where are you learning about sex and/or consent—for example, media and entertainment sources, educators, parents, doctors, public health campaigns, or religious leaders? Which of these sources do you trust and why? What advice resonates with you?

Luca saw the look Zoe gave her. "What?" she defended herself. "It's not slut-shaming if she's an actual slut, right?"

Zoe kept glaring. "No, it still is."

"Oh, lighten up," said Luca breezily. "You know I'm just kidding. Besides, sleeping with someone just so they won't sleep with someone else is a dumb idea."

"Wait, Gabriella. Did Paul say that he would sleep with someone else if you said no to him?" Zoe's brows contracted.

"He'd better not have said that." Luca's normally sweet features twisted into a scowl.

"No," said Gabriella. "He didn't say that, exactly."

Zoe looked fiercer than ever. "What did he say, exactly?"

"He said he loved me!" Gabriella exclaimed. "He wanted our first times to be together. He said he would rather be with me

TALK ABOUT IT

- Would you ever call someone a "slut?" If so, under what circumstances? How would you feel if someone used that word to describe you?

- What do you think Luca's motives are for calling Caitlin a slut?

- Slut-shaming, or disrespect toward someone because how they express their sexuality might not fit social norms, happens more to females than males. What is your opinion of this double standard? Of slut-shaming in general?

"He said he loved me!" Gabriella exclaimed.

than anyone else, and he hoped I would show him I felt the same!"

Luca whistled. "Wow, that's . . . something."

Zoe gritted her teeth. "That's it. I was on the fence about Paul, but now I can say he's a terrible boyfriend. You should dump his slimy little butt the first chance you get."

"But why?" said Gabriella. "I don't see what he's done that's so awful. I love him and he loves me. I don't want to break up with him. I just need to decide whether I'm going to sleep with him. Can we get back to that question, please?"

"I don't see what he's done that's so awful. I love him and he loves me."

TALK ABOUT IT

= Why was the way Paul asked Gabriella to sleep with him a clear violation of her consent? How might he have asked her to sleep with him in a way that respected her boundaries?

= Why do you think Zoe thinks Paul is a terrible boyfriend and that Gabriella should break up with him? Do you agree or disagree? Why or why not?

= If you were Gabriella, what would you do? Why would you make that choice?

ASK THE

EXPERT

Consent is an ongoing process between people. It must be continually asked for and given. Just because someone wants to spend time or have sex with you today doesn't mean they will want to in five days, or even in five minutes. Consent is specific to only the activity that's been discussed. Just because someone is OK with kissing doesn't mean they're OK with other touching. Thirdly, consent has to be freely given. If you are feeling manipulated, shamed, teased, or guilt-tripped into something, that's a clear sign your boundaries are being violated. That's why consent can't be given when there's a clear imbalance of power, like between a boss and employee, a teacher and student, or an adult and a teen—because the person with less power might not feel that they can say no. And consent can only be given when the person giving consent is awake, aware, and fully willing. Someone who is passed out or woozy because of drugs, alcohol, or tiredness cannot give consent. Finally, consent can be revoked at any time. If a person who has said "yes" says "no" at any time, that "no" immediately, unquestionably counts. That person doesn't have to explain, justify, or apologize for their decision.

GET **HEALTHY**

- Consent is crucial. Be honest and verbal about what you do and don't want. A partner should only do what you've given them specific permission to do.

- Choose safety. It's possible to get pregnant or catch a sexually transmitted infection (STI) with just one instance of unprotected sex.

- If you decide to have penis-in-vagina sex, using a birth control method like the pill or an IUD in addition to a condom is the most effective way other than abstinence to prevent both pregnancy and STIs.

- Find a partner who respects you in all things and doesn't just want sex. If your partner ever belittles you, mistreats you, or pushes you to do anything you're not comfortable with, they're not the right sexual partner *or* someone who deserves to be in a relationship with you.

THE LAST WORD FROM **CARRIE**

Regardless of who your partner is, how long you've been together, or what your friends want you to do, your decision to have or not have sex—or any other interaction with your partner—is up to you. Your sexuality, like the rest of you, is developing and maturing during your teen years. You may find that what you want from a relationship and how you think of your own sexuality changes drastically as you move toward adulthood. So don't rush yourself. Reach out to adults you trust when you need help and advice. Honor, respect, and take care of yourself now and make the best decisions you can for your body, emotions, and health. You'll set yourself up for a healthy, fulfilling sex life well past your teen years.

A SECOND
LOOK

There's no question that adolescence is a high-intensity, high-pressure time of life. Jordan, Amaya, Destiny, Trina, Mika, Jasmine, Kiki, and Gabriella all found themselves in stressful situations. Whether they were dealing with pressure from family, boys, friends, school, or a combination, they each had the opportunity to handle their stress in a positive, healthy way. They did it through mindfulness, self-compassion, building self-awareness, taking care of and honoring themselves and others, and getting help and advice from friends, mentors, parents, and professionals when they needed it.

When I was a kid, there was a popular bumper sticker that said something like, "Be patient! Life isn't finished with me yet." Although this would sound trite if applied to an adult—and also like a bad excuse for immature behavior—for a teenager, it holds a lot of truth. You *are* far from finished yet as a person, so you can afford to be patient with yourself as your body and mind grow a little more every day.

On your worst days, remember that someday your hormones will settle down, the parts of your brain that aren't that active at the moment will wake up again, and everything will make more sense. On your best days, celebrate your good friends, your incredibly malleable brain, and all the qualities that make you the unique and wonderful person you are. And on both bad days and good, treat yourself with the same kindness that you lavish on the friends you love the most.

HERE'S TO YOU! BEST WISHES FOR
AN AMAZING ADOLESCENCE,
CARRIE

PAY IT
FORWARD

Taking care of yourself is important. Discovering what makes you feel your best is a journey that changes throughout your life. Now that you know what to focus on, you can pay it forward to a friend too. Remember the Get Healthy tips throughout this book, then take these steps to get healthy and get going.

1. Be kind to yourself. Learn about self-compassion and put its principles and exercises into practice. Honor and celebrate who you are now.

2. When you're feeling stressed in the moment, use a breathing or mindfulness exercise to counteract your stress response and help you feel grounded and in control.

3. Track your moods and your menstrual cycle. Note the times of month when you feel good (usually right after your period ends) and when you feel not-so-good (before your period starts). When you know a moody day is coming, find ways to care for yourself and avoid extra stress if possible. You can warn others about your moods, too, to head off possible conflict.

4. Remember that exercise, diet, and sleep are the three pillars of stress relief.

5. Take advantage of your teenage brain's plasticity to get really good at something you have a natural aptitude for and enjoy doing. This will increase your confidence in yourself and counterbalance pressure in other areas of your life.

6. Challenge your negative thinking patterns and replace them with self-affirming ones.

7. Do the best you can and then let it go. That goes for school, sports, relationships, and decisions about your future—basically, everything. View mistakes as learning opportunities while keeping in mind the old saying "Perfect is the enemy of good." Also this one: "You've got your whole life ahead of you."

8. Don't hesitate to ask for help for yourself or for a friend. Parents, teachers, school counselors, clergy, doctors, and mental health professionals are all potential resources you can draw on in a crisis or before you hit the point of crisis.

GLOSSARY

adolescence
The period between childhood and adulthood when a young person grows up, beginning at the onset of puberty.

anxiety
A feeling of fear about a future event.

consent
The process of obtaining explicit and clear permission to cross someone's physical boundaries. Consent must be given without pressure, guilt, or manipulation; refers only to the specific activity for which it's obtained; and can be taken back at any time.

depression
A common but serious mental illness characterized by lasting sadness and anxious feelings that interfere with your normal daily activities.

hormone
A regulatory substance that sparks an action, such as growth, digestion, or sexual maturation, in a tissue or organ.

lethargic
To feel tired and slow.

obsess
To constantly think about.

period
An occurrence that happens to sexually mature females about once a month where there is a flow of blood from the lining of a woman's uterus.

PMS (premenstrual syndrome)
Bodily and emotional changes caused by hormone fluctuations as the menstrual period approaches.

puberty
The beginning of physical maturity when a person becomes capable of reproducing sexually.

ADDITIONAL
RESOURCES

SELECTED BIBLIOGRAPHY

Greenland, Susan Kaiser. *Mindful Games: Sharing Mindfulness and Meditation with Children, Teens, and Families.* Shambhala, 2016.

Hemmen, Lucie, PhD. *Parenting a Teen Girl: A Crash Course on Conflict, Communication, and Connection with Your Teenage Daughter.* New Harbinger, 2012.

FURTHER READINGS

Jones, Keith. *Mental Health Information for Teens, Fifth Edition.* Omnigraphics, 2017.

Tompkins, Michael A., and Jonathan R. Barkin. *The Relaxation and Stress Reduction Workbook for Teens: CBT Skills to Help You Deal with Worry and Anxiety.* New Harbinger, 2018.

ONLINE RESOURCES

To learn more about coping with stress and pressure, please visit **abdobooklinks.com** or scan this QR code. These links are routinely monitored and updated to provide the most current information available.

For more information on this subject, contact or visit the following organizations:

The American Academy of Child and Adolescent Psychiatry (AACAP)

3615 Wisconsin Ave. NW
Washington, DC 20016-3007
202-966-7300
aacap.org

AACAP is an advocacy, education, and research organization that supports the healthy development of children, adolescents, and families. It also provides resources for child and adolescent psychiatrists.

The Center for Adolescent Health

Johns Hopkins Bloomberg School of Public Health
615 N. Wolfe St.
Baltimore, MD 21205
410-955-3543
jhsph.edu/research/centers-and-institutes/center-for-adolescent-health

The Center for Adolescent Health helps urban youth to become healthy and productive adults. The center partners with community organizations to identify the needs and strengths of young people and promote their health and well-being.

INDEX

ABOUT THE
AUTHOR

CARRIE MYERS

Carrie Myers is a native Californian with roots in Hawaii, Japan, Okinawa, and the Philippines. She lives in New York City with her husband and three *hapa* (mixed Asian and Caucasian) children, ages 17, 14, and eight. After earning her PhD in English and American Literature and teaching at various schools including New York University, Barnard College, and City Seminary of New York, she now works as a spiritual director, writer, and editor. She enjoys music, summer barbecues with family and friends, trying different kinds of bubble tea, and making people feel at home. She is currently obsessed with baby Holland Lop bunnies, perhaps the cutest balls of fluff on the planet (although reportedly quite destructive to your furniture).